Make Your Own
Crochet
Animals

Make Your Own
Crochet
Animals

CREATE YOUR OWN UNIQUE ANIMALS AND PATTERNS

Karolina Knapek

WHITE OWL

Published in Great Britain in 2022 by
WHITE OWL BOOKS
An imprint of
Pen & Sword Books Ltd
Yorkshire - Philadelphia

© 2022 Karolina Knapek

ISBN 978 1 52677 3 821

Book Design by Dominic Allen

Printed and bound in the UK,
by Short Run Press Limited, Exeter

Pen & Sword Books Limited incorporates the imprints of Atlas, Archaeology, Aviation, Discovery, Family History, Fiction, History, Maritime, Military, Military Classics, Politics, Select, Transport, True Crime, Air World, Frontline Publishing, Leo Cooper, Remember When, Seaforth Publishing, The Praetorian Press, Wharncliffe Local History, Wharncliffe Transport, Wharncliffe True Crime and White Owl.

For a complete list of Pen & Sword titles please contact:
PEN & SWORD BOOKS LIMITED
47 Church Street, Barnsley, South Yorkshire, S70 2AS, England
E-mail: enquiries@pen-and-sword.co.uk
Website: www.pen-and-sword.co.uk

Or
PEN AND SWORD BOOKS
1950 Lawrence Rd, Havertown, PA 19083, USA
E-mail: Uspen-and-sword@casematepublishers.com
Website: www.penandswordbooks.com

FSC
www.fsc.org
MIX
Paper from
responsible sources
FSC® C014540

CONTENTS

ACKNOWLEDGEMENTS..................6

INTRODUCTION 7

FROM THE AUTHOR 9

CHAPTER ONE   THE BASICS 12

CHAPTER TWO   ANIMAL KEY RINGS 31

CHAPTER THREE   ANIMAL ORNAMENTS 47

CHAPTER FOUR   TOYS 72

CHAPTER FIVE   LET'S PLAY 'DRESS UP'................91

CHAPTER SIX   COMFORTERS................................. 104

CHAPTER SEVEN   CHRISTMAS BAUBLES...................124

CONCLUSION 143

ABBREVIATIONS 144

ACKNOWLEDGEMENTS

I would like to thank my son for being a constant source of inspiration for my projects; he is only a toddler but has the ability to spark in me some wonderful ideas when he tries to imitate animal noises and through play. This book wouldn't have happened without the amazing support of my inspiring husband David; he has been a rock to me throughout writing this book, as my dad was diagnosed with cancer and was going though the treatment as I wrote. I couldn't have done it without you, David, my love, I thank you.

To my parents Janina and Zenon who even though they were going through a very rough and stressful time were always there to cheer me on. I love you.

And to my parents-in-law Sandra and Steve: I want to thank you for your wonderful support and help and for always being there to look after Dylan when I needed some more free time to write and work on perfecting the patterns.

Also thank you to my wonderful friends Aimee and James, I can always count on you to have good advice, kind words and unquestionable friendship.

I am so blessed to have all of you around me; thank you from the bottom of my heart.

INTRODUCTION

Creating new things has been a passion of mine since I was a little girl. For as long as I can remember, I always had some creative project going on, whether it was crocheting, knitting, candle-making, woodwork, macrame, or sewing. My grandmother had a major influence on me when it came to making things yourself and reusing things you have around you. When I stayed at my grandparents' house, I made things with my grandma who gave me tips and advice: from how to hold the crochet hooks to be comfortable and efficient, to what size yarn will work best for a project. I could not thank her enough for teaching me how to crochet. We started with simple scarves with wool – using yarn from her old sweater – that was so much fun as a small child: destroying something and giving new life. Crocheting became something I would dip in and out of at different times in my life, almost completely forgetting about it whilst studying at university, and then picking it back up again upon moving to London fourteen years ago. London was such an inspiring place to be for me; there are so many creative opportunities for crafts that it encouraged me to pick up the hook again, driven by selling my wares on market stalls. I found that instead of making scarves and tea cosies I had a fresh perspective on what crocheting could be; I discovered I could create something fresh, fun and enticing: it's known as amigurumi crochet. My first commission was a close friend's baby shower; I wanted to create something unique, and not just purchase a plastic toy that would get forgotten about in a landfill. I made a toy/soother that her little bundle of joy will be able to play with for many years. It's a small dinosaur holding a little blanket that she can hold and play with, perfect for little hands. It was such a hit I soon had more ideas about how I could create similar things that would resonate with young mothers, be personal and bring joy and comfort to little babies.

I started from bear and bunny patterns that I found online, but in time I moved on to making my own patterns based on photos or finding inspiration in the natural world. I began creating teethers, key rings, Christmas baubles and more. This book can be seen as a jumping-off point; you will follow along with my tried and tested patterns, making all sorts of animals – and soon you'll be customising them to your own preferences. The possibilities are endless. Now my friends and clients are sending me images or ideas of the things that they would like to have made and every single time it's something new and exciting.

This book is an amazing opportunity for me to share my designs and hopefully inspire more people to create their own animals. In each chapter you will learn to make a different animal, as well as learning a new pattern. I will show you how to make key rings, toys, Christmas decorations and ornaments, as well as how to customise them with accessories like hats and moustaches.

FROM THE AUTHOR

REUSE, REDUCE, RECYCLE

I can't say that enough. I really dislike waste. I am a firm believer that you can reuse and limit waste to a minimum and I try to do this with everything that I make.

> *'More than 300,000 tonnes of used clothing go to landfill in UK every year, textiles release methane, a greenhouse gas, as they degrade in landfill.'*
>
> **WRAP THE WASTE CHARITY**

It is absolutely deplorable. We can do so much better! In this regard I would like to share few tips that I use, where possible, to reduce the waste whilst creating my animals. For example, we almost always have a long tail left with a finished piece that we attach to the main body. I always have a little 'scrap/waste' box for my yarn where I put all the cuttings. After a few completed patterns you will accumulate a fair amount of scrap wool which can be used to help with the stuffing of your animal. I use the yarn together with the polyester filling inside the body so I never throw it into the bin.

It's quite satisfying to see it go in, knowing it has not gone to waste. In addition to this, I reuse old pillows, old jumpers and scraps of cloth from other projects to help with bulking out the filling for my project.

Before opening the casing of a pillow, I put it through the washing machine as per manufacturer's instructions to avoid any shrinkage and bulkiness – as when this happens it will be hard to achieve a smooth body for the animal. Once washed and smelling lovely, I rip the cushion up and stuff all my animals. The cushion case can be used for either storing the polyester filling or by turning it into a dishcloth; it works well as glass lens cleaner or general dusting cloth … and the best thing is that you just pop it in the wash and reuse, reuse, reuse. Oh, and let's not forget that it saves you a little bit of money!

One thing that I try to do when making animals is to use as small a number of plastic components as possible; I much prefer sewing eyes using yarn on the animal. Sometimes it's unavoidable – for example when I'm making a Christmas bauble I have to use a plastic ball for the base; it is light enough to not fall from the tree, and it won't break that easily. I tried using Styrofoam but found that it became too easily misshapen.

I know most of you have this already, but I think it's worth mentioning the need for: a small tool container. For example, I use a lunch box with clips. It's a slightly fancier-looking piece of Tupperware and I have had it since I first thought about creating animals and other creatures using this crochet method. I keep only the essential things that I use all the time: a few different sized hooks; sewing and tapestry needles; 4-pin needles, which I keep on a small ball that I crocheted long time ago; some stitch markers, scissors; and a small tape measure.

YARN THAT I USE

I think it's fair to say that I am yarn addicted. I have so much of it, but believe you can never have too much; nothing stops a project in its tracks faster than running out of the materials you need. I find it really helps with a project to use the right kind of yarn – for some projects you might want something thick and bold, for others something delicate. For me, it makes the work go so much faster and it's obviously more enjoyable when the yarn is easy on your fingers. For the projects described in this book, I would recommend that the best type of yarn is naturally dyed, organic 100 per cent cotton yarns; they are so soft and really easy to work with – and they come in such a variety of colours that you can find something suitable for any project. They are also easy to procure from your local craft shop. Really though, use whatever you have, make sure to use the right size hook and you will be away. Using thicker yarn will simply result in a bigger animal, but will not mean it has any more stitches – the pattern will still apply.

CHAPTER ONE

THE BASICS

STITCHES

For the most part we will be using a single crochet pattern working continuously in a spiral, placing a marker at the beginning of each round. We will also work with a half double crochet stitch. I like to use ring-type markers as they are very easy to slide in and out. My patterns are mainly worked in both loops, but there will be a few occasions when we will be crocheting in either the front or the back of the loop.

The only time when we will be using half double crochet will be when creating tentacles for the octopus.

Here is a quick refresher on the stitches we will be using in this book:

SINGLE CROCHET

Insert your hook through the first loop, wrap the yarn over the hook then pull though both loops.

DOUBLE CROCHET

Wrap the yarn over your hook then insert the hook through the loop, wrap the yarn over your hook again, pull through, wrap the yarn over, pull through two loops, wrap the yarn over, pull through two loops.

TRIPLE CROCHET

Wrap the yarn twice over your hook then insert though the loop, wrap the yarn over and pull though, wrap the yarn over again and pull through the two loops, wrap the yarn over and pull though two loops, finally wrap the yarn over and pull through the last two loops.

HALF DOUBLE CROCHET

Wrap the yarn over, then insert the hook through the loop, wrap the yarn over and pull through three loops.

3

4

5

MAGIC CIRCLE

With the end part of the yarn facing inside the palm of your hand, wrap the yarn over your two fingers making a cross, now insert the hook under both strands, wrap and then pull through the second strand under the first, then twist the hook, wrap the yarn over and pull though the loop.

EXPERIENCE

The patterns in this book are fairly straightforward but you will need to have a bit of knowledge on how to crochet to begin with: making a chain, magic circle, single crochet, increase, decrease, slip stitch as well as how to increase and decrease stiches.

Some parts of the patterns can be fiddly, such as when making foxes' ears or crocheting around the plastic ball when making Christmas tree decorations, I will guide you through – take it slowly and be sure to follow the patterns carefully. I often found that my second and third attempt resulted in a neater creation. If some of this feels unfamiliar, there are plenty 'how to' videos online, which I recommend as it is easy enough to follow along with the few simple steps. I have videos for each on my You Tube channel – Mustard Cat Studio.

DECREASING

When it comes to decreasing there are many different ways of doing it. Decrease is abbreviated 'dec' but it can also be called 'two together' – which is essentially what you are doing. When working decrease, you start single crochet in one stitch, and leave it unfinished while you start single crochet in the adjacent stitch. Finishing them both together to create one single crochet across the two stitches. This feels quite complicated right?!!

I like to use an alternative way called the 'Invisible Decrease Method'. It goes as follows:

Insert the hook in the front loop, leaving it unfinished while you insert the hook in the adjacent front loop.

This method results in a neater pattern and has the advantage of making it almost impossible to see where you made the decrease. This is specifically useful when making Christmas baubles as we are working with smooth plastic bauble – any lumps and bumps will be especially visible in this case, whereas when working with just polyester filling you can get away with a bit of untidiness.

STUFFING YOUR ANIMALS

I mainly use polyester filling for most of my projects, as it is easily accessible and fairly low cost, although as mentioned you can use old pillows and supplement with your scrap pieces of yarn. For some creations I use old fabric from other projects; this is helpful if I want the object to be particularly firm, and although it's more fiddly using fabric it is worth it in the end. I prefer not to use any implements to push the filling in – I find that it's better to have a soft touch to ensure that there is no stretching of the yarn. In every project, stuffing the animal will come just before finishing the last few stitches – I prefer to stuff as I go so that when an arm or a leg is finished it's ready to be attached.

CHAPTER TWO

ANIMAL KEY RINGS

DUMBO OCTOPUS

When I first saw the Dumbo octopus on a nature documentary, I fell in love. They are such cute, intelligent little creatures with such personality, I knew I had to try to make one straightaway. A perfect size for a key ring, they are a great way to keep track of spare keys or fobs, and as I learned in the documentary they can change colour so this makes for a fantastic opportunity to experiment. This pattern is easy to follow and quick to make. This is a fun little project that should take approximately forty-five minutes to complete. You will need to know how to make single crochet, how to increase and make a magic circle as described in the first chapter.

The head and tentacles are made in one continuous piece, working in a single crochet and increases pattern. Tummy and ears will be crocheted separately and joined together later.

HEAD

Row 1	magic circle	(6st)
Row 2	inc in each st	(12st)
Row 3	1sc │ inc │ 2sc │ inc │ 2sc │ inc │ 2sc │ inc │ 1sc │	(16st)
Row 3	3sc │ inc │ 3sc │ inc │ 3sc │ inc │3sc │ inc │	(20st)
Row 4	4sc │ inc │ 10sc │ inc │ 4sc │	(22st)
Row 5	7sc │ inc │ 5sc │ inc │ 8sc │	(24st)
Row 6	work even	(24st)

At this point insert eyes with at least eight stitches between them. Make sure that the safety clip is pushed all the way in.

Row 7-9   work even   (24st)

Row 10   work even but only in front loop   (24st)

This is where we start creating the lovely joined tentacles (it looks a bit like a skirt!) that the Dumbo octopus has. I have made only two rows for this project, but don't let that stop you – you can add as many as you like. To do this simply follow the pattern as described below, and then for each new row you add two more stitches (so Row 13 would be 7 | 4 x inc; Row 14 would have 9 | 4 x inc; and so on.) I find you can go really crazy with this, and it's very satisfying to see the little wavy lines get more and more exaggerated; they look really pretty.

Row 11   3sc | 4 x inc | 3sc | 4 x inc | 3sc | 4 x inc | 3sc | 4 x inc | 3sc | 4 x inc | 3sc | 4 x inc | 3sc | 4 x inc | 3sc | 4 x inc | (48st)

Row 12   5sc | 4 x inc | 5sc | 4 x inc | 5sc | 4 x inc | 5sc | 4 x inc | 5sc | 4 x inc | 5sc | 4 x inc | 5sc | 4 x inc | 5sc | 4 x inc | (72st)

TUMMY

Here is where you can go wild with colours; don't get me wrong white is just fine but when you add a lovely contrasting colour it makes the whole piece 'pop' and makes it so much more special, interesting and one of a kind. I tend to choose my body colour first and leave the tummy to the end.

When you insert the eyes you can really give your creature some character and expression. The one I have shown here is a cute little grumpy character, by putting the eyes in higher, lower or at a different angle you will quickly get a feel for what you find works. I like to place the eyes relatively low in the pattern to accentuate its baby features – keeping the eyes small and far apart helps create the illusion that this octopus is not fully grown.

Row 1	magic circle	(6st)
Row 2	inc in each st	(12st)
Row 3	1sc ⏐ inc ⏐ 1sc ⏐ inc ⏐ 1sc ⏐ inc ⏐ 1sc ⏐ inc ⏐ 1sc ⏐ inc ⏐ 1sc ⏐ inc ⏐	(18st)
Row 4	2sc ⏐ inc ⏐ 2sc ⏐ inc ⏐ 2sc ⏐ inc ⏐ 2sc ⏐ inc ⏐ 2sc ⏐ inc ⏐ 2sc ⏐ inc ⏐	(24st)

Sew both together with your needle going through the front loop on the tummy (closer to you) and then through the back loop on the body.

EARS – MAKE TWO

The ears are simple to make and so adorable. They make the whole look complete.

Chain 3 and fold in half, tie both ends together, pin them to the head before sewing to ensure you are happy with the placement. Make sure they are spaced quite a bit apart to achieve optimum cuteness.

Now add the key chain, using small jewellery pliers (if you don't have jewellery pliers you could use a thin pair of scissors or even a metal pen), spread the jump ring apart, then use tweezers to hold it while you thread it though the loop.

The Dumbo octopus is ready. I hope you had fun making this little guy and enjoyed giving him some character. I find that every time I make one I end up giving it a slightly different expression – they will always be one of a kind no matter how many times you make them. For me this is what I enjoy the most about this kind of project, every time is a unique creation, ready to go out into the world to look after some keys.

WHALE

This little whale is another small, quick project that can be both useful and enjoyable. As you can imagine, in our household we have lots of animals chained to our keys. It's so easy to find them, and it saves lots of 'where is the key to the shed?!' as it's much easier to see a brightly coloured whale than a lone shed key – they are also light and fit perfectly in the hand.

Body, tummy and fins are crocheted separately. Body is worked in a ball pattern using single crochet repeats and increases. Tummy will be made in a circle pattern using the single crochet and increase method.

YOU WILL NEED:

- Grey wool
- Blunt-ended tapestry needle
- Stitch marker
- Pliers
- Polyester filling
- Key ring
- A pair of safety eyes – 5mm
- Crochet hook – 4.5mm

BODY

Row 1	magic circle	(6st)
Row 2	inc in each st	(12st)
Row 3	1sc | inc | 2sc | inc | 2sc | inc | 2sc | inc | 1sc |	(16st)
Row 3	3sc | inc | 3sc | inc | 3sc | inc | 3sc | inc |	(20st)
Row 4	4sc | inc | 10sc | inc | 4sc |	(22st)

Row 5-9   work even   (22st)

Row 9   in this row insert eyes

I usually fold the piece in half and place the eyes in the middle of each half to get the most equal distance.

TUMMY

I have ensured that the body and the tummy have an equal number of stitches so sewing them together is easier and looks neater. I have chosen a white yarn for this but don't feel you are limited to my choice here. Experiment!

Row 1	magic circle	(6st)
Row 2	inc in each st	(12st)
Row 3	1sc | inc | 1sc | inc | 1sc | inc | 1sc | inc | 1sc | inc | 1sc | inc |	(18st)
Row 4	2sc | inc | 2sc | inc | 6sc | inc | 2sc | inc | 2sc |	(22st)

Once you have finished the tummy, you can stuff your whale with polyester filling and sew body and tummy together. This is the time when you can use your offcuts and reuse what you would normally throw away.

FINS

The fins can be a bit tricky, especially when you come to join them with the body, but don't worry, what I find that helps is to use a one size smaller crochet hook to get into those tight spaces.

FRONT FINS

Starting from the back (last loop of the whale's body) count five stitches, join your chains to the body, then

sc | ch1 | sc | ch1 | sc | sl st | (weave the ends)
– repeat on the other side

BACK FIN

This you will have to make separately from the body and sew it on right in the middle of the back. You can use the end of the round of the top of the body as a guide to where to start sewing.

ch4 | 2dbl | sl st | ch4 | 2dbl |

CHAPTER THREE

ANIMAL ORNAMENTS

HIPPO

This hippo is a great project to move on to after you have mastered the key rings shown in the previous chapter. There are no fiddly bits in this project, but you will find that it will take a bit more time to create – approximately an hour and a half, due to the larger size of the hippo. I find it makes for a fantastic fabric weight; I've stuffed its tummy with small pebbles to give some weight as well as the usual polyester filling. A hippo makes a fantastic Christmas stocking gift! You can also make it into a door stopper if you use a much thicker yarn (such as T-shirt yarn which is heavy and really bulky) then stuff him with one large pebble with some polyester filling around it so you can't see though; a perfect little chubby door stopper is ready.

YOU WILL NEED:

- Teal & white cotton yarn
- Blunt-ended tapestry needle
- Stitch marker
- Polyester filling
- A pair of safety eyes – 4mm
- Crochet hook – 4.5mm

Head, body, legs, ears and tail are worked separately in a single crochet and increase pattern.

When crocheting the head you will start with a regular ball pattern, which will be the mouth section. Then you will decrease to create the head part where you will insert eyes and attach ears. If you have been successful the body will look a bit like a pear.

The body is worked in a continuous ball pattern, with a few rows that are crocheted with the same amount of stitches – this is to lengthen the body.

Legs are crocheted in two parts: first we are going to make the base of the foot that will be in a different colour from the pillar of the leg, which will be joined together and worked in a continuous single crochet pattern.

HEAD

Row 1	magic circle	(6st)
Row 2	inc in each st	(12st)

Row 3	1sc ǀ inc ǀ 2sc ǀ inc ǀ 1sc ǀ inc ǀ 2sc ǀ inc ǀ 1sc ǀ	(17st)
Row 4	2sc ǀ inc ǀ 3sc ǀ inc ǀ 2sc ǀ inc ǀ 3sc ǀ inc ǀ 3sc ǀ	(21st)
Row 5	4sc ǀ inc ǀ 6sc ǀ inc ǀ 6sc ǀ inc ǀ 2sc ǀ	(24st)

Row 6-7   work even   (24st)

| *Row 8* | 2sc \| dec \| 6sc \| dec \| 6sc \| dec \| 4sc \| | (21st) |
| *Row 9* | 3sc \| dec \| 3sc \| dec \| 2sc \| dec \| 3sc \| dec \| 2sc \| | (17st) |

Row 10   dec ǀ 1sc ǀ dec ǀ 2sc ǀ dec ǀ 1sc ǀ dec ǀ
2sc ǀ dec ǀ 1sc ǀ   (12st)

Row 11-13   work even   (12st)

Insert the eyes just as you will finish row 12

Row 14   decrease three times   (6st)

Now cut a long tail and sew the last six stitches to close the gap and tuck the remaining tail inside the body.

EARS – MAKE TWO

Ears are made in single crochet. Once you have created the circle pull the yarn tight and make a knot. That way you will find it a bit easier to sew the ears on and pin them to the head.

| *Row 1* | magic circle | (4st) |

Pin to the head first to make sure they are evenly spaced.

Get sewing! Cut the excess yarn and tuck the rest inside the head.

BODY

The body is made using single crochet stitch; it is worked in a continuous ball pattern, with six rows worked even in the middle of the body to give it some length. You can of course omit these six rows and simply have a large ball, or you could even work in more than six rows to create a much longer hippo. If you have the patience you might even be able to make a lovely draft excluder!

Row 1	magic circle	(6st)
Row 2	inc in each st	(12st)
Row 3	1sc | inc | 1sc | inc | 1sc | inc | 1sc | inc | 1sc | inc | 1sc | inc |	(18st)

Row 4	2sc | inc | 2sc | inc | 2sc | inc | 2sc | inc | 2sc | inc | 2sc | inc | (24st)
Row 5	3sc | inc | 3sc | inc | 3sc | inc | 3sc | inc | 3sc | inc | 3sc | inc | (30st)
Row 6	4sc | inc | 4sc | inc | 4sc | inc | 4sc | inc | 4sc | inc | 4sc | inc | (36st)

Rows 7-12	work even	(36st)

Row 13	4sc dec 4sc dec 4sc dec 4sc dec 4sc dec 4sc dec	(30st)
Row 14	work even x 1	(30st)
Row 15	3sc dec 3sc dec 3sc dec 3sc dec 3sc dec 3sc dec	(24st)

| Row 16 | 2sc dec 2sc dec 2sc dec 2sc dec 2sc dec 2sc dec | (18st) |
| Row 17 | 1sc dec 1sc dec 1sc dec 1sc dec 1sc dec 1sc dec | (12st) |

Row 18   decrease three times   (6st)

Pull the remaining yarn tight and tuck inside the body.

You can now pin the head and the body together – exciting! Almost there…

FEET – MAKE FOUR

The feet are worked in a circle starting from the base. I have used a different colour for the sole of the foot. You will then chain one and attach it to the circle, working in a single crochet a few rows up to create a cylinder leg. For the feet I only use a little bit of polyester filling just to make sure they are steady and chubby.

BOTTOM OF THE FEET

Row 1	magic circle (white yarn)	(5st)
Row 2	inc in each (white yarn)	(10st)

CYLINDER PART OF THE FEET

Rows 3-7   work even in the different colour   (10st)

TAIL

Chain 4 then cut a long tail, next fold in half and tie a knot. Pin it to the body and get sewing. Once you have finished tuck the leftover yarn inside the body.

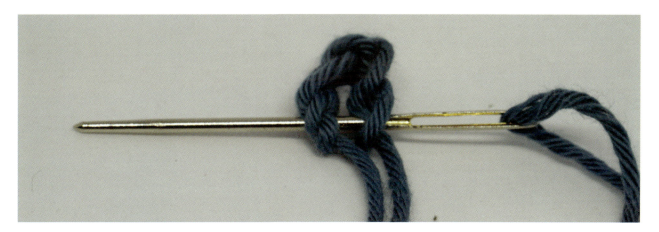

OCTOPUS

At the beginning of my journey into crocheting animals, the octopus was the first animal I tried to make. I have my husband to thank for this, he asked if I could make one similar to the one he has tattooed on his arm. I was very pleased with my first attempt, and was surprised that I could create this creature without looking at a pattern. Of course, I had made quite a few things in crochet before but this was my first animal. I quickly made several more and wrote down the pattern so I could have a quick reference. The pattern that we will make here is the result of a few improvements and tweaks that I have made over the years to that first octopus. I have made this octopus so many times and have given it many different personalities and expressions. In Chapter 5, I will show you how, with a simple hat and moustache, you can create a fun character.

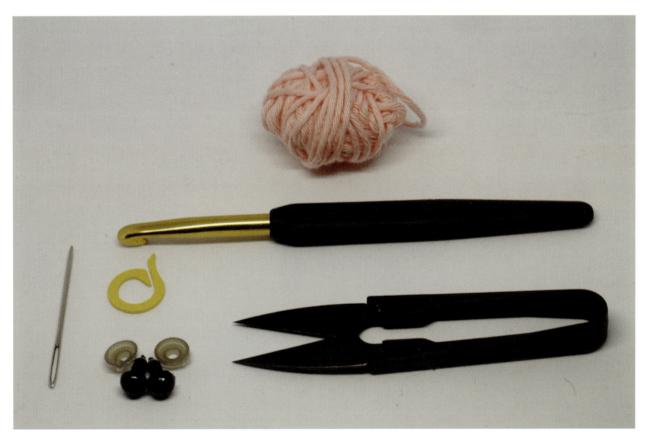

The head is crocheted separately from the tentacles and tummy. You will work in single crochet repeats and increases; the tentacles are crocheted directly from the tummy and they are worked with single chains and four half double crochet repeats in each chain. This is what creates the lovely spiral effect.

HEAD

| Row 1 | magic circle | (6st) |
| Row 2 | inc in each st | (12st) |

| Row 3 | 1sc | inc | 2sc | inc | 1sc | inc | 2sc | inc | 1sc | inc | | (17st) |

| Row 4 | 1sc | inc | 3sc | inc | 2sc | inc | 3sc | inc | 2sc | inc | 1sc | | (22st) |

Row 5   2sc | inc | 5sc | inc | 4sc | inc | 5sc | inc | 2sc | (26st)

Row 6   4sc | inc | 7sc | inc | 8sc | inc | 4sc | (29st)

Row 7   7sc | inc | 9sc | inc | 9sc | inc | 1sc | (32st)

Row 8   13sc | inc | 18sc | (33st)

Insert the eyes spacing them at least ten stitches apart.

Row 9   work even   (33st)

Row 10   18sc | dec | 13sc | (32st)

Row 11   1sc | dec | 9sc | dec | 9sc | dec | 7sc | (29st)

Row 12   4sc | dec | 8sc | dec | 7sc | dec | 4sc | (26st)

| Row 13 | 2sc | dec | 5sc | dec | 4sc | dec | 5sc | dec | 2sc | (22st) |
| Row 14 | 1sc | dec | 2sc | dec | 3sc | dec | 2sc | dec | 3sc | dec | 1sc | (17st) |

TUMMY

The tummy is worked in a circle; it has the same number of stitches as the main body of the octopus to allow an almost seamless join.

| *Row 1* | magic circle | (6st) |
| *Row 2* | 2sc \| inc \| 2sc \| inc \| 2sc \| inc \| 1sc \| inc \| inc \| | (17st) |

TENTACLES – MAKE EIGHT

Start from the marker – ch12, and then second st from the back. Make 4hd repeat in each stitch.

Pin the head to the tummy and sew together, going through front loops only.

Sew together.

Lovely pink octopus is ready.

CHAPTER FOUR

TOYS

✕✕✕✕✕✕✕✕✕✕✕✕✕✕✕✕

SLOTH

Sloths are such cute animals, and they are perfect for amigurumi; their long limbs hanging from trees make for an excellent method of creating a hanging animal – by attaching magnets to the arms and legs. This one is cute and light and will hang from radiators and fridges alike and I hope you will have as much fun making this little guy as I did! It is also fun finding places for him to hide in plain sight. The first sloth I made was a Christmas present for a friend – he still hangs out on the fridge to this day.

YOU WILL NEED:

- Light/dark brown yarn & cream yarn
- Tapestry needle
- Stitch marker
- Magnet rings
- A pair of safety eyes – 7mm
- Crochet hook – 4.5mm

The head, face, body, legs and arms are all crocheted separately.

The head is worked in a continuous ball pattern with single crochet, increase and decrease repeats.

The face consists of two separate parts that will be attached together by safety eyes and all will be sewn to the head.

The body is crocheted in a continuous ball pattern with two rows in the middle, which are worked with the same number of stitches.

The legs and arms are crocheted in the same pattern until each measures approximately 8 cm and at the beginning of each when it measures 2cm we will insert the magnets.

HEAD

Row 1	magic circle	(6st)
Row 2	inc in each	(12st)
Row 3	1sc │ inc │ 2sc │ inc │ 2sc │ inc │ 2sc │ inc │ 1sc │	(16st)
Row 4	3sc │ inc │ 3sc │ inc │ 3sc │ inc │ 3sc │ inc │	(20st)
Row 5	4sc │ inc │ 10sc │ inc │ 4sc │	(22st)

Row 6-8	work even	(22st)
Row 9	4sc │ dec │ 10sc │ dec │ 4sc │	(20st)
Row 10	dec │ 3sc │ dec │ 3sc │ dec │ 3sc │	(16st)
Row 11	1sc │ dec │ 2sc │ dec │ 2sc │ dec │ 2sc │ dec │ 1sc │	(12st)

BODY

Row 1	magic circle	(6st)
Row 2	inc in each	(12st)
Row 3	1sc ǀ inc ǀ 2sc ǀ inc ǀ 1sc ǀ inc ǀ 2sc ǀ inc ǀ 1sc ǀ inc ǀ	(17st)
Row 4	2sc ǀ inc ǀ 3sc ǀ inc ǀ 3sc ǀ inc ǀ 3sc ǀ inc ǀ 2sc ǀ	(21st)
Row 5	3sc ǀ inc ǀ 6sc ǀ inc ǀ 6sc ǀ inc ǀ 3sc ǀ	(24st)
Row 6	5sc ǀ inc ǀ 5sc ǀ inc ǀ 6sc ǀ inc ǀ 5sc ǀ	(27st)
Row 7-8	work even	

Row 9	5sc ǀ dec ǀ 6sc ǀ dec ǀ 5sc ǀ dec ǀ 5sc ǀ	(24st)
Row 10	3sc ǀ dec ǀ 6sc ǀ dec ǀ 6sc ǀ dec ǀ 3sc ǀ	(21st)
Row 11	2sc ǀ dec ǀ 3sc ǀ dec ǀ 3sc ǀ dec ǀ 3sc ǀ dec ǀ 2sc ǀ	(17st)

Row 12	dec │ 1sc │ dec │ 2sc │ dec │ 1sc │
	dec │ 2sc │ dec │ 1sc │	(12st)
Row 13	dec in each	(6st)

Thread the needle through the outside part of the chain and pull tight to close the gap.

FACE

The face is worked in an oval shape.

Row 1		(ch6)
Row 2	3sc │ inc │ 4sc │ inc │ 1sc │	(10st)
Row 3	1sc │ inc │ inc │ inc │ 3sc │ inc │ inc │ 2sc │	(16st)

DARK RIM FOR THE EYES

Row 1   8sc | inc | 5sc | inc | 6sc | (23st)

Secure the darker rims on the face with safety eyes as shown. Make sure that the long tail is pointed away from the face and slightly downward to create the sleepy sloth face markings.

Pin to the head and get sewing.

ARMS & LEGS
- MAKE FOUR TOTAL

Row 1   magic circle 5st – work round until the piece measures 8cm; you can now insert the magnet in each limb. Make sure you pull the circle tight to ensure that the magnet stays secured.

Now you can start pinning pieces together. It is a good idea to have the head turned to the side, this way when he is holding on to a fridge, radiator or curtain rail you will still be able to see his face.

And here he is!

BUNNY

The bunny is a classic design that makes for an excellent gift for all ages. It's easily customizable, meaning you can create almost any character you like with this pattern. Tailoring the bunny to exactly what you need, with the flexible arms and legs, means the bunny can be posed into any situation. With a cute little face and a lovely fluffy tail, this is one of my favourite characters to make. He will be taking part in dressing up later in the book; I think he looks great in hats!

YOU WILL NEED:

- Orange/pink/black and fluffy white yarn
- Blunt-ended tapestry needle
- Tapestry needle
- Stitch marker
- Scissors
- Crochet hook – 4.5mm

Head, body and legs are crocheted in one piece using a single crochet and increase method: the head and body create an oval shape, the legs are based on a cylinder shape with the sole worked separately and then joined to the cylinder. The ears and tail are worked separately using a single crochet and increase method.

BODY

Row 1	ch12, second chain from the hook make an inc ⎮ 10sc ⎮ 2x inc ⎮ 9sc ⎮ inc ⎮ (PM) (27st)

Row 2	inc ⎮ 11sc ⎮ inc ⎮ 1sc ⎮ inc ⎮ 11sc ⎮ inc ⎮ (31st)

Row 3   1sc | inc | 12sc | inc | 1sc | inc |
12sc | 2x inc | (36st)

Row 4-28   work even   (36st)

EARS

Row 1	magic circle	(6st)
Row 2	inc in each	(12st)
Row 3	3sc | inc | 3sc | inc | 3sc | inc |	(15st)
Row 4-8	work even	(15st)
Row 9	dec | 5sc | dec | 6sc |	(13st)
Row 10-11	work even	(13st)
Row 12	dec | 4sc | dec | 5sc |	(11st)

FEET

Divide the body. Pin/mark three chains in the middle on both sides of your work; each leg should have fifteen stitches.

Start crocheting around the fifteen stitches and do so for six rows. This part is a bit tricky – you will see some holes – but don't worry we will sew everything up at the end.

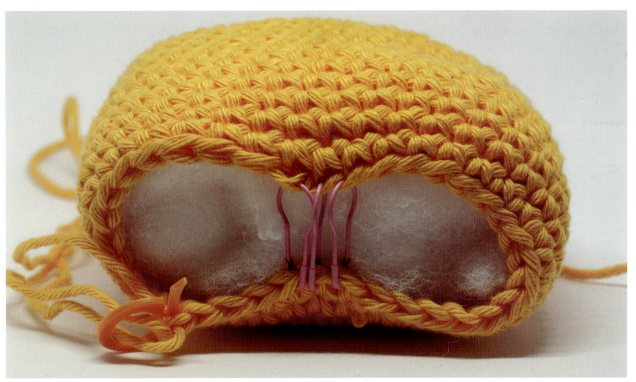

With the second leg you will have to cut the yarn and start on the other side with the new loop and again go around the fifteen stitches for six rows.

BOTTOM LEG

| *Row 1* | magic circle | (8st) |
| *Row 2* | 7x inc ‖ 1 ‖ | (15st) |

Pin the bottom of the legs so they are easier to sew.

Now let's start putting the bunny together.
First pin the ears and sew.

NOSE

In the pictures you can see that I have used a temporary nose – the purpose of this is to establish exactly where the middle of the face is. This helps with locating the eyes and mouth later. I like to use a colour that is markedly different from that I plan to use so that it is obvious. I work over the temporary nose stitches four times – you can do as many as you like here to create a smaller or larger nose. If you do more the nose will be more apparent and will create a cute bobble.

EYES

Having marked out the temporary nose with scrap yarn it is now time to place the eyes. Using your tapestry needle and black yarn, go under two stitches and pull through.

Then go over and back.

Then at about a 45-degree angle, insert the needle above the first stitch.

Next going back to the first stitch, weave the yarn in between the body.

FLUFFY TAIL

Row 1   magic circle   (8st)

Row 2   work even

With a needle, thread through the front loops and pull tight; here you can see I have added a bit of polyester filling along with some scraps.

CHAPTER FIVE

LET'S PLAY 'DRESS UP'

In this chapter you will be able to mix and match different hats and moustaches, creating all kinds of looks for your creations so far. Want to make your octopus posh? Give him a top hat. Feel as though your bunny needs a bit of shade from the sun? A large summer hat will do the job.

Here are my patterns for two styles of moustache and five different hats. These can be adjusted to create all kinds of styles in any colours you like. I hope you will have as much fun as I did.

SMALL BOWLER HAT

TOP OF THE HAT

The top of the hat is worked in a half ball shape; starting with magic circle with increases and then continuing in the circle pattern down until the desired length is achieved.

Row 1	magic circle	(8st)
Row 2-5	work even	

Weave both tails into the hat; to keep the hat firm and to help it keep its shape, you will need a bit of polyester filling for the top.

RIM OF THE HAT

The rim of the hat is worked in continuous circle pattern using single crochet and increases starting with magic circle method.

Row 1	magic circle	(10st)
Row 2	inc in each	(20st)

TOP HAT

TOP OF THE HAT

The top of the hat is worked in a tube shape; starting with magic circle with increases and then continuing in the circle pattern will achieve this. Inserting your hook in the first row only in the back loops, then working down until the desired length.

Row 1	magic circle	(6st)
Row 2	increase in each sc	(12sc)
Row 3	work even but only in back loops	
Row 4-10	work even	

You can make the top hat as tall as you like; some characters will look better with a different size hat, so adjust to your taste by working even for more than ten rows for a longer hat, or stop at four rows for a short one. When you fill it you can decide how stiff and rigid you want it to be – sometimes a floppy top hat can be lots of fun; but for a more pristine, polished look, stuff with lots of filling.

RIM OF THE HAT

The rim of the hat is again worked in a continuous circle pattern using single crochet and increases starting with magic circle method.

Row 1	magic circle	(6st)
Row 2	increase in each	(12st)
Row 3	inc ⎪ 1sc ⎪ inc ⎪ 1sc ⎪ inc ⎪ 1sc ⎪ inc ⎪ 1sc ⎪ inc ⎪ 1sc ⎪ inc ⎪ 1sc ⎪	(18st)
Row 4	2sc ⎪ inc ⎪ 2sc ⎪ inc ⎪ 2sc ⎪ inc ⎪ 2sc ⎪ inc ⎪ 2sc ⎪ inc ⎪ 2sc ⎪ inc ⎪ 2sc ⎪	(24st)
Row 5	work even	

Cut long tail and weave in the ends under the hat.

LADY'S SUMMER HAT

TOP OF THE HAT

The top of the hat is worked in a half ball shape, which will be achieved by starting with magic circle with increases, and then continuing in the circle pattern down until we make it the desired length.

Row 1	magic circle	(6st)
Row 2	inc in each	(12st)
Row 3	work even twice	

Weave both tails into the hat. You will need a bit of polyester filling for the top to make it nice and stable.

RIM OF THE HAT

The rim of the hat is worked in continuous circle pattern using single crochet and increases starting with magic circle.

Row 1	magic circle	(6st)
Row 2	inc in each	(12st)
Row 3	1sc ⎸ inc ⎸ 1sc ⎸ inc ⎸ 1 sc ⎸ inc ⎸ 1sc ⎸ inc ⎸ 1sc ⎸ inc ⎸ 1sc ⎸ inc ⎸	(18st)
Row 4	inc each	(36st)
Row 5	inc ⎸ 2sc ⎸ eighteen times	(56st)

Now join both top and bottom of the hat using a tapestry needle. For the red rim, you can use any type of yarn – I used the same cotton yarn I use for all my animals as I always have an abundance – but use any colour you like to personalise the hat further. To begin with, wrap the yarn twice around the bottom part of the hat then push the needle down all the way through the hat so it's visible when you flip it up. Repeat with the other end of the yarn going though the same spot, then tie both together underneath to secure it.

GREY LADY'S HAT

RIM OF THE HAT

The rim of the hat is worked in continuous circle pattern using single crochet and increases starting with magic circle method.

Row 1	magic circle	(6st)
Row 2	increase in each sc	(12st)
Row 3	inc │ 1sc │ inc │ 1sc │ inc │ 1sc │ inc │ 1sc │ inc │ 1sc │ inc │ 1sc │	(18st)
Row 4	2sc │ inc │ 2sc │ inc │ 2sc │ inc │ 2sc │ inc │ 2sc │ inc │ 2sc │ inc │ 2sc │	(24st)
Row 5	work even	(24st)

TOP OF THE HAT

Row 1	magic circle	(6st)
Row 2	1sc │ inc │ 1sc │ inc │ 1sc │ inc │	(9st)
Row 3	work even in the back loops only	(9st)
Row 4	work even in both loops	(9st)

Cut long tail. Stuff with a bit of polyester or any offcuts of yarn that you might have left over from other projects.

STEP 1

Pin top and rim/bottom together for easier sewing.

STEP 2

Use the long tail from the top part of the hat to sew two together. Weave in the tail from the rim between loops.

First go through the next loop and then follow the loops underneath …

… all the way to the centre. That will give you an almost invisible finish.

RIBBON

When I wrap the ribbon, I flip the rim to get better access to the top part of the hat …

… just where the top and bottom have been sewn together, then I wrap the ribbon around. To create the bow …

… fold it over and pin it down to make sure everything stays in place. Then get a sewing needle and red thread ready. With the needle, go from underneath the hat to through the top, then through all three pieces of ribbon. This is followed by making three French knots to secure the ribbon, which will create a lovely flower arrangement. Adding both completes the look and gives it character.

FRENCH KNOT

You will need both hands for this. With your non-needle hand, pinch the thread a few inches from where it exits the hat. Hold it tight with the hand not holding the needle. Now place the needle in front of the stretch thread. The needle has to be in front of the thread, not behind it. This will ensure that the thread doesn't become

wonky. Wrap the tread around the needle six times – you can wrap it around more times if you like to make it more bulky. Continue the tension with your non-needle hand to prevent unwrapping. Next, re-insert the tip of the needle just next to (but not in) the same exit point of the hat (if you insert the needle in the same spot you will lose your knot). With your non-needle hand (that is pinching the length of the thread), give a little downward tug with so it's all nice and tight. Slide the needle down to make a little bundle against the surface of the hat. Now you can push the needle all the way through.

SOMBRERO

The top part of this hat is a cone shape, and is worked in a continuous circle pattern using single crochet and increases. It can be a bit tricky at the start as it is not always easy to increase in the circle with such a small chain, but if you keep your loops looser for those first three it will be much easier to thread the hook though them to make the initial increases.

Row 1	magic circle	(3st)
Row 2	increase in each	(6st)
Row 3	1sc | inc | 1sc | inc | 1sc | inc |	(9st)
Row 4 -5	work even	
Row 6	2sc | inc | 2sc | inc | 2sc |	(12st)
Row 7	3sc | inc | 3sc | inc | 3sc |	(15st)
Row 8	work even	(15st)

Cut the long tail and stuff the cone with either polyester filling or any scraps and offcuts you might have left over from other projects.

RIM OF THE HAT

The rim of the hat is worked in a continuous circle pattern using single crochet and increases, starting with the magic circle.

Row 1	magic circle	(6st)
Row 2	increase in each	(12st)
Row 3	inc | 1sc | inc | 1sc | inc | 1sc | inc | 1sc | inc | 1sc | inc | 1sc |	(18st)
Row 4	2sc | inc | 2sc | inc | 2sc | inc | 2sc | inc | 2sc | inc | 2sc | inc | 2sc |	(24st)
Row 5	4sc | inc | 8sc | inc | 6sc | inc | 2sc |	(27st)
Row 6	8sc | inc | 4sc | inc | 6sc | inc | 6sc |	(30st)
Row 7	work even	(30st)

Cut the long tail after the end of the row then weave the end inwards.

Row 8 add a red rim by chaining one on the hook, and joining it to the main piece. Work even, using the single crochet method for the whole length of the row. Cut the long tail and weave the end on the inside part of the hat.

Pin top and rim together – for easier sewing use the long tail (photo) from the top part of the hat to sew two together. Weave in the tail from the rim in between loops. First go through the next loop and then follow the loops underneath all the way to the centre to give you an almost invisible finish.

For the red and green pattern: wrap both threads individually, one on top of another – I used a smaller crochet hook to pull the ends of each colour inside the hat – and then tighten them underneath to secure them.

You'll notice that with these hats, in addition to creating some exquisite fancy dress items, we've got the essential building blocks of just about any geometrical shape: a cylinder, cone and a half ball. With these shapes you could use the patterns to create all kinds of things. Want to give your character an ice-cream cone? Create a half ball, give it a short frilly rim – choose your flavour, then make a cone shape in light brown and sew them together.

MOUSTACHES

Both moustaches are worked on a chain using single, double, half double and triple crochet, and also using slipstitch method.

GENTLEMAN'S MOUSTACHE

This moustache works in many situations – paired with a bowler hat or top hat you can complete a character. Keep your stitches fairly loose to keep things easier; this will also help with keeping the lovely curly shape.

Row 1   (ch15)

Row 2   sl st | sl st | 1sc | 1hdc | 1dc | 1tc | 1dc | sl st | ch1 | 1dc | 1tc | 1dc | 1hdc | 1sc | sl st – weave ends

HANDLEBAR MOUSTACHE

For the handlebar moustache you will find that loose stitches will help to keep the process easy, as they can get a bit fiddly. This moustache works well with any of the hats, the sombrero would be the obvious choice, but if you go for a bowler hat in brown, you have yourself a cowboy – just use less stuffing to give the bowler hat a divot in the top.

Row 1   (ch18)

Row 2   sl st | 1sc | 1sc | 1hdc | 1hdc | 1dc | 1dc | 1tc | sl st | 1tc | 1dc | 1dc | 1hdc | 1hdc | 1sc | 1sc | sl st – weave in the ends

CHAPTER SIX

COMFORTERS

I have a little boy who at the time of writing this book is a 1-year-old. I have, of course, made him all sorts of toys, teddy bears and hanging mobiles and such. The two described here are my absolute favourites. With the rabbit, the intention was to give him something that he would hold on to and play with on car journeys; every time we get in the car, we give him the rabbit, and every time we give him the rabbit he knows we are going somewhere in the car. He likes to point and waggle the rabbit at buses and pedestrians as they go whooshing past the window. We find it certainly provides a calming effect as babies at this age love routine. The panda was going to be the toy he would hold in the buggy, but after dropping him in one too many puddles, he now sits clean and washed in his bedroom window. You can't win them all, and he is just too cute to keep getting muddy.

RABBIT

The body and head are made in a rectangle shape; they are continuous – there is no neck so you won't be sewing the head to the body. We will work it in one piece using single crochet and increase method. Legs, arms, ears and tail are worked separately using single crochet and both increase and decrease method. This rabbit is very baby/newborn friendly – it does not require plastic safety eyes and they will love the floppy arms and legs. In addition to this, we will make a pouch for the polyester filling – this will

prevent any filling from falling out, as well as allowing us to shape the body better. Because of the long shape of the body, sometimes polyester filling can bulk up in one part, so some massaging will be required to smooth it out – especially if, like me, you are using filling from an old pillow.

YOU WILL NEED:

- Light grey, pink, white and black yarn
- Cotton fabric 15.5cm x 15.5cm
- Tapestry needle
- Sewing needle and thread
- Stitch marker
- Polyester filling
- Crochet hook – 4.5mm

Row 1   ch10, in the second chain from the end make an increase, then 7sc, 2 x inc (in the same st), then 7sc and inc in last st (22st) total.

Work the piece even until it measures 12cm; don't cut off the tail as we will use it to work continuously with one leg.

Cut out a square 15.5cm by 15.5cm of cotton fabric. I like to use an old shirt for this; as long as the material is not stretchy it will be perfect (stretchy fabric will bulge in places when you stuff it with the filling).

Fold the fabric in half on the wrong side (i.e. the side that does not have the pattern printed on it) and stitch two sides, leaving only the bottom part open to allow room to insert the stuffing. Reverse the fabric and start stuffing. It is entirely up to you how firm you want the rabbit to be – on this occasion I made it quite firm, knowing that the arms, legs and ears will be long and flexible enough to be waggled. Sew up the bottom of the fabric and place one stitch marker in the middle of the crocheted part to separate the legs.

STEP 1

Fold the fabric on the wrong side then sew the two sides.

STEP 2

Reverse and stuff.

STEP 3

Place inside the crochet piece and sew the bottom.

STEP 4

Place the marker in the middle to separate the legs – each leg will have ten stitches.

LEGS

Continue working the first leg until it measures 12cm in single crochet pattern; this first leg will be the easiest as the yarn is worked continuously from the body.

The other you will have to chain one on the hook and join the main work and work ten stitches in a round until the leg measures 12cm.

There will be a gap between the legs but don't worry, use a tapestry needle and a bit of leftover yarn of the same colour and stitch the gaps. There is no need to use the hook as the gaps will be very small. Once you are done stuff the ends inside the body.

ARMS - MAKE TWO

Row 1   magic circle   (8st)

Work even until the piece measures 12cm, then decrease three times, cut the long tail and make the other arm the same way. Pin both arms to body and sew on.

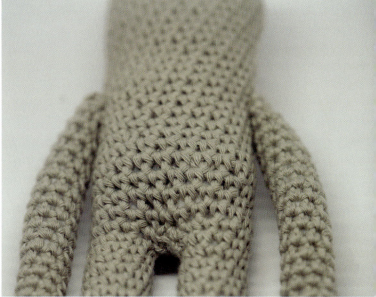

EARS - MAKE TWO

Row 1   magic circle   (6st)

Row 2   increase in each st   (12st)

Row 3   3sc | inc | 3sc | inc | 3sc | inc | (15st)

At this point, I place a small stitch marker to indicate where the row began so that way I don't have to take the marker out at each row and generally it's just easier and faster to work.
   Work until the piece measures 9cm.

| *Row 1 after 9cm* | dec ‖ 3sc ‖ dec ‖ 3sc ‖ dec ‖ 3sc ‖ | (12st) |
| *Row 2 after 9cm* | dec in each st | (6st) |

Cut long tail and make the other ear.
Now pin both ears to the head and sew on.

EYES

Mark out a temporary nose with scrap yarn to help make sure the eyes are evenly spaced, then using a tapestry needle and black yarn go under two stitches and pull through.

Then go over and back.

Then at about a 45-degree angle insert the needle above the first stitch.

Then go back to the first st and weave the yarn in between the body.

NOSE

Sew the nose on in the same place as the temporary nose; try to be as neat as possible. Going under about two stitches and then working over those two stitches about four times, you can do more repeats or less for a different shape nose.

Once you are happy with the nose, tuck in the ends and we are nearly done.

TAIL

Row 1   magic circle   (6st)

Cut the long tail, weave the tail in the outside loops only, and pull tight, pin to the body and sew on.

PANDA

Head, body, arms, legs, ears and eyes are made separately using the single crochet decrease and increase method. For this piece I used polyester filling as well as scraps from a shirt – since this pattern is ball-shaped it is easy to stuff without lumps and bumps. As this toy is designed for little babies I don't advise using any plastic safety eyes. In addition to this, make sure to leave a long tail for each part so when it comes to sewing you will have enough excess to ensure a very strong hold for each component. This will ensure the longevity of the toy as they do tend to get thrown about a bit.

YOU WILL NEED:

- White and black yarn
- Tapestry needle
- Stitch marker
- Polyester filling
- Crochet hook – 4.5mm

HEAD

Row 1	magic circle	(6st)
Row 2	increase in each	(12st)
Row 3	inc | 1sc | inc | 1sc | inc | 1sc | inc | 1sc | inc | 1sc | inc | 1sc |	(18st)
Row 4	2sc | inc | 3sc | inc | 2sc | inc | 3sc | inc | 3sc | inc |	(23st)
Row 5	5sc | inc | 3sc | inc | 3sc | inc | 5sc | inc | 3sc |	(27st)
Row 6	4sc | inc | 5sc | inc | 6sc | inc | 9sc |	(30st)
Row 7	3sc | inc | 4sc | inc | 6sc | inc | 4sc | inc | 4sc | inc | 3sc | inc |	(36st)
Row 8	5sc | inc | 6sc | inc | 4sc | inc | 7sc | inc | 6sc | inc | 3sc |	(41st)
Row 9	3sc | inc | 4sc | inc | 3sc | inc | 5sc | inc | 5sc | inc | 8sc | inc | 7sc |	(47st)
Row 10-12	work even	(47st)
Row 13	7sc | dec | 8sc | dec | 5 | dec | 5dec | 3sc | dec | 4sc | dec | 3sc |	(41st)
Row 14	3sc | dec | 6sc | dec | 7sc | dec | 4sc | dec | 6sc | dec | 5sc |	(36st)
Row 15	dec | 3sc | dec | 4sc | dec | 4sc | dec | 6sc | dec | 4sc | dec | 3sc |	(30st)
Row 16	9sc | dec | 6sc | dec | 5sc | dec | 4sc |	(27st)
Row 17	3sc | dec | 5sc | dec | 3sc | dec | 3sc | dec | 5sc |	(23st)

Cut long tail.

Row 18   join black yarn to the work by chaining one on
          the hook and now work as follows –
          dec | 3sc | dec | 3sc | dec | 2sc | dec |
          3sc | dec | 2sc | (18st)

This will give us an almost invisible join between head and body.
    Cut the long tail and stuff the head with polyester filling and scraps.

BODY

Start with black yarn.

Row 1   magic circle   (6st)

Row 2   increase in each   (12st)

Row 3   inc | 1sc | inc | 1sc | inc | 1sc | inc | 1sc |
          inc | 1sc | inc | 1sc | (18st)

Row 4   2sc | inc | 3sc | inc | 2sc | inc | 3sc | inc |
          3sc | inc | (23st)

Row 5   5sc | inc | 3sc | inc | 3sc | inc | 5sc |
          inc | 3sc | (27st)

Row 6   4sc | inc | 5sc | inc | 6sc | inc | 9sc | (30st)

Row 7   3sc | inc | 4sc | inc | 6sc | inc | 4sc | inc |
          4sc | inc | 3sc | inc | (36st)

Row 8   5sc | inc | 6sc | inc | 4sc | inc | 7sc | inc |
          6sc | inc | 3sc | (41st)

Row 9   work even

Row 10   3sc | inc | 4sc | inc | 3sc | inc | 5sc | inc |
5sc | inc | 8sc | inc | 7sc | 1sc | (48st)

At this point we will join the work with white yarn, on the last stitch in the round we will add one more single crochet; this will allow us to have a neat and tidy join between two colours.

Row 11	work even 46sc then make a decrease	(47st)
Row 12-21	work even	(47st)
Row 22	7sc | dec | 8sc | dec | 5 | dec | 5dec | 3sc | dec | 4sc | dec | 3sc |	(41st)
Row 23	3sc | dec | 6sc | dec | 7sc | dec | 4sc | dec | 6sc | dec | 5sc |	(36st)
Row 24	dec | 3sc | dec | 4sc | dec | 4sc | dec | 6sc | dec | 4sc | dec | 3sc |	(30st)
Row 25	9sc | dec | 6sc | dec | 5sc | dec | 4sc |	(27st)
Row 26	3sc | dec | 5sc | dec | 3sc | dec | 3sc | dec | 5sc |	(23st)
Row 27	dec | 3sc | dec | 3sc | dec | 2sc | dec | 3sc | dec | 2sc |	(18st)

STUFF THE BODY.

Row 28	1sc | dec | 1sc | dec | 1sc | dec | 1sc | dec | 1sc | dec | 1sc | dec |	(12st)
Row 29	decrease six times, cut long tail, using a tapestry needle go through back loops only, pull tight to create a nice finish, tuck in leftover yarn.	

LEGS & ARMS
- MAKE TWO OF EACH

Row 1	magic circle	(6st)
Row 2	increase in each	(12st)
Row 3	inc ┃ 1sc ┃ inc ┃ 1sc ┃ inc ┃ 1sc ┃ inc ┃ 1sc ┃ inc ┃ 1sc ┃ inc ┃ 1sc ┃	(18st)
Row 4-5	work even	(18st)
Row 6	decrease six times	(12st)

Work even until the piece measures 7cm, then decrease six times to achieve 6st, cut the long tail and pull tight. Repeat for the other three pieces.

Pin all to the body on the sides.

Make sure you sew them on by going under the arms and legs – this will ensure they hug the body and stay nice and secure.

EARS - MAKE TWO

Row 1	magic circle	(6st)
Row 2	increase in each	(12st)
Row 3	inc | 1sc | inc | 1sc | inc | 1sc | inc | 1sc | inc | 1sc | inc | 1sc |	(18st)
Row 4	work even	(18st)
Row 5	decrease six times	(12st)

Cut long tail.

EYES - MAKE TWO

| *Row 1* | magic circle | (6st) |
| *Row 2* | increase in each | (12st) |

Cut long tail.

STEP 1

Put the needle under the corner of the eye with white yarn.

STEP 2

Thread the needle on the other side of the eye and go under in about two stitches space.

STEP 3

Tuck the ends inside the head.

NOSE

Insert the needle under two stitches and over, repeat three times so the nose is nice and perky.

CHAPTER SEVEN

CHRISTMAS BAUBLES

Christmas is my favourite time of the year; it sparks so many ideas for festive creations. There are so many wonderful things you can put on your Christmas tree – I just wish my ceiling were higher so I could have a taller tree. I always start decorating the house in the last weekend of November so by the time it's December I only have the final touches left. I always like to find a way to make my decorations unique; these patterns certainly are just the ticket!

You will have so much fun creating this little decoration, it's unusual and original. I hope it will bring a smile to everyone's faces and make a great addition to any tree.

RACCOON

The idea for a raccoon as a decoration came from a cartoon – obviously they are usually associated with trash and burglars, but when I saw this creature rolling around with his fat little belly, I decided it could be the perfect design for amigurumi. I was at first unsure how it would be received, but I quickly found that it added a stylish, kooky, hip angle to any decoration. They have proved popular with family friends and customers.

This bauble is worked in four parts: body, mask, ears and nose using single crochet increase and decrease method, the body is worked continuously around a plastic bauble.

YOU WILL NEED:

- Grey/white/black wool
- Tapestry needle
- Stitch marker
- Pair of safety eyes
- Plastic bauble - 7cm
- Crochet hook – 5mm

BODY

Row 1   magic circle   (6st)

Row 2   inc in each   (12st)

Row 3   1sc | inc | 1sc | inc | 1sc | inc | 1sc | inc | 1sc | inc | 1sc | inc | (18st)

Row 4   2sc | inc | 2sc | inc | 2sc | inc | 2sc | inc | 2sc | inc | 2sc | inc | (24st)

Row 5   3sc | inc | 3sc | inc | 3sc | inc | 3sc | inc | 3sc | inc | 3sc | inc | (30st)

Row 6	4sc | inc | 4sc | inc | 4sc | inc | 4sc | inc | 4sc | inc | 4sc | inc |	(36st)
Row 7	16sc | inc | 19sc |	(37st)
Row 8-11	work even	(37st)
Row 12	19sc | dec | 16sc |	(36st)
Row 13	4sc | dec | 4sc | dec | 4sc | dec | 4sc | dec | 4sc | dec | 4sc | dec |	(30st)
Row 14	3sc | dec | 3sc | dec | 3sc | dec | 3sc | dec | 3sc | dec | 3sc | dec |	(24st)
Row 15	2sc | dec | 2sc | dec | 2sc | dec | 2sc | dec | 2sc | dec | 2sc | dec |	(18st)
Row 16	1sc | dec | 1sc | dec | 1sc | dec | 1sc | dec | 1sc | dec | 1sc | dec |	(12st)
Row 17	decrease three times	(6st)
Row 18	stitch in the front loops and pull tight	

EARS - MAKE TWO

Row 1	magic circle	(5st)
Row 2	increase in each stitch	(10st)
Row 3-5	work even	(10st)

When you finish making the ears, make sure you leave a generous tail for when you sew them on. Sew on white tips by going from under the ear and pushing the needle through the top – out and round the back. Staying just at the tip of the ears, repeat this at least three times to achieve even coverage.

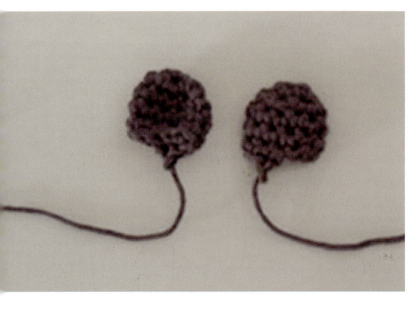

EYES - MAKE TWO
- AND BLACK 'MASK'

The mask is worked in a continuous oval pattern using single crochet and increases.

Row 1   ch5, from the next stitch, inc | 2 |
         2 x inc | 2 | inc | (12st)

Row 2   inc | 4 | inc | inc | 5 | (15st)

Insert safety eyes (cut the stems off the eyes as they will be too long to fit on the bauble) Next from the top of one side of the 'mask' ch9 with white yarn.

Leave a long tail for both the white and black piece, as it is always easier to secure the pieces.

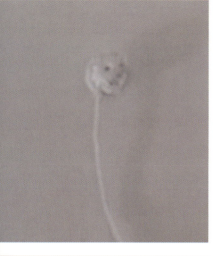

NOSE

The nose is worked on magic circle with single crochet increases in the loop.

Row 1   magic circle   (8st)

Cut the long tail and, using a tapestry needle, go through the front loops and pull tight.

Leave a long tail.

Now add a black nose tip by threading the needle just under the middle of the white part, then threading over about four or five times.

You should now have all the pieces to construct your bauble. The difficult part is over. All that is left is the assembly of the bauble. Using pin needles, attach the parts into place; this way you can see how he will look before you start sewing the pieces on. It is easier to sew the parts on when the pins are still in, but be careful as it is easy enough to accidentally prick your fingers, so go slowly and take your time.

To finish up, sew on the bauble topper, and trim any loose threads and then tuck them under. You have now completed a lovely raccoon bauble!!

FOX

This is one of my absolute favourites, the classic red fox; if I could, I would have crocheted foxes everywhere in the house in all shapes and sizes. This creation began life as a brooch; I found the brooch to be very popular at markets, and decided to upgrade it to make a larger design – the red fox bauble has so far proven to be my fastest-selling item. Contrasting on a green Christmas tree, it looks fabulous peeking out from behind the fronds. The sunburnt orange colours contrast very well with a luscious green tree. Add a hat and a moustache and you have a rather fetching gentleman fox. The pattern itself you will find is easy enough to adjust for almost any cat or dog – you can use the patterns shown in this book to take this basic bauble design and create personalised animal baubles – and I really mean personalised - everybody knows someone with a pet they hold dear, what better Christmas present than a recreation of their favourite pet that can be brought out every year?

YOU WILL NEED:

- Orange/white/black wool
- Blunt-ended tapestry needle
- Stitch marker
- Pin needles
- Plastic bauble - 6cm
- Crochet hook

You will work this bauble in three parts, body, ears and nose, using single crochet, increase and decrease method. The body is worked continuously around a plastic bauble.

HEAD

Row 1	magic circle	(6st)
Row 2	inc in each	(12st)
Row 3	inc ǀ 1 ǀ inc ǀ 1 ǀ inc ǀ 1 ǀ inc ǀ 1 ǀ inc ǀ 1 ǀ inc ǀ 1 ǀ	(18st)
Row 4	2sc ǀ inc ǀ 2sc ǀ inc ǀ 2sc ǀ inc ǀ 2sc ǀ inc ǀ 2sc ǀ inc ǀ 2sc ǀ inc ǀ 2sc ǀ	(24st)
Row 5	3sc ǀ inc ǀ 3sc ǀ inc ǀ 3sc ǀ inc ǀ 3sc ǀ inc ǀ 3sc ǀ inc ǀ 3sc ǀ inc ǀ 3sc ǀ	(30st)
Row 6	4sc ǀ inc ǀ 4sc ǀ inc ǀ 4sc ǀ inc ǀ 4sc ǀ inc ǀ 4sc ǀ inc ǀ 4sc ǀ inc ǀ 4sc ǀ	(36st)
Row 7	8sc ǀ inc ǀ 27sc ǀ	(37st)

Row 8	work even	(37st)
Row 9	27sc ‖ dec ‖ 8sc ‖	(36st)
Row 10	dec ‖ 4sc ‖ dec ‖ 4sc ‖ dec ‖ 4sc ‖ dec ‖ 4sc ‖ dec ‖ 4sc ‖ dec ‖ 4sc ‖	(30st)
Row 11	dec ‖ 3sc ‖ dec ‖ 3sc ‖ dec ‖ 3sc ‖ dec ‖ 3sc ‖ dec ‖ 3sc ‖ dec ‖ 3sc ‖	(22st)
Row 12	dec ‖ 2sc ‖ dec ‖ 2sc ‖ dec ‖ 2sc ‖ dec ‖ 2sc ‖ dec ‖ 2sc ‖ dec ‖ 2sc ‖	(18st)

Row 13   dec | 1sc | dec | 1sc | dec | 1sc | dec |
1sc | dec | 1sc | dec | 1sc | (12st)

Row 14   decrease three times   (6st)

You will be left with 6st, thread the needle though the outside loops all the way around, and pull tight.

EARS - MAKE TWO

Row 1	magic circle	(3st)
Row 2	inc in each	(6st)
Row 3	1sc │ inc │ 1sc │ inc │ 1sc │ inc │	(9st)

Row 4	2sc │ inc │ 2sc │ inc │ 2sc │	(12st)
Row 5-8	work even	(12st)

Flatten the ear so it gets nice pointy look.

WHITE PART OF THE EAR

Row 1   magic circle – 3st – in the same last stitch ch1, in the next one hdc and in the next ch1, pull together and cut the long tail and make a knot.

Sew the two pieces together, taking the white part, and placing it on the base of the ear. With your tapestry needle and white thread go from underneath the ear where you have the opening, and push the needle through both, then go round the white part. Once you have gone through the shape, thread the needle back inside the ear – you do not need to tie it, as you will just push the offcuts inside the ear with your finger, then flatten back the ear. Now repeat for the other ear.

Now you can add the pattern of the top of the fox's ears with black yarn. Take your needle and go through the middle of the ear, push your needle just at the top and go round the top, repeat four times.

Pin your ears to the fox to make sure they are spaced evenly, and get sewing. Remember to tuck in all the leftover yarn - if it's a bit too long you can always cut and reuse the ends when stuffing another project.

NOSE

The nose is worked in a magic circle with single crochet increases.

Row 1   magic circle   (6hdc)

Pull a little bit, cut long tail. With the needle inserted through the back loops, pull tight.

With the black yarn, thread the needle from the back through to the middle of the nose. Create a V-shape when you do the two first initial threads, and then fill in the blank space – use as many repeats as you need to make sure there are no white spaces left.

Still going through the middle create a little V-shape.

Fill in the white space to create a cute little nose.

Pin to the fox before sewing to make sure you are happy with the placement and get sewing; try to thread your needle just under the nose; do not leave any thread to the side of the nose, as this way we will keep the nose flush to the bauble.

EYES

Insert the needle two stitches above the nose line, take the thread parallel for three stitches, and then take a 45-degree upwards angle for one stitch.

Once you come back to where you started, cut some of the thread and tuck the rest underneath.

CONCLUSION

I hope that you have enjoyed working with my patterns. It is clear that with just a few simple shapes it is possible to create all sorts of cute and fun projects, with more and more complex shapes coming from the simple ones. With these first steps under your belt, you can combine and reuse the patterns in all sorts of ways – for example, did you notice that the rabbit when flipped upside down still looks like a bunny, but with a completely different character? You can make lions and tigers and bears by making smaller ears, or perhaps make a pig, using the hippo pattern for its body and the tentacle pattern from the octopus for its curly tail. You can create a whole zoo using the patterns shown in this book; it's absolutely possible to use the techniques shown to create almost anything – the next step is to find inspiration. A good place to start is with giving gifts. Have a nephew that likes birds, or a niece that loves ice cream? Try making it with crochet. You'll find immense satisfaction when you discover you can now create anything you can think of with just a few simple stitches. Reusing an old jumper will only make the experience even more personal.

ABBREVIATIONS

sc	single crochet
ch	chain
dec	decrease
inc	increase
tc	treble crochet
dc	double crochet
hdc	half double crochet
sl st	slip stitch
PM	place marker